Transforming Trash

Pat Quinn

Learning Media

Contents

1. A Mountain of Mess

If we could see all the stuff that we throw out, we probably wouldn't like what we saw. It would make a small (and very smelly) mountain of mess. We'd find food scraps, paper, clothing, metal, glass, and body waste (the kind that goes down the toilet). Then there's the trash created from industry and farming, when chemicals, ashes, dead animals, and plants are thrown out, and from leftover building materials.

After about 2 years, each person's trash mountain would weigh about as much as a large rhinoceros.

The average amount of solid trash produced per person in countries like the United States, the United Kingdom, and Canada is about 4 pounds a day, which adds up to about 1,500 pounds a year for each of us.

How do we move the mountain?

One way is to get rid of it!

Around 90 percent of the solid trash that is produced gets spread onto the land or buried in landfills. Most of the remaining 10 percent is burned in commercial incinerators. A small amount is allowed to rot into garden compost.

Trash Disposal Method	Pluses	Minuses
Landfill (throw it on the land and squash it down) 	• Cheap, all that's needed is unused land areas and a bulldozer. • Gets rid of a lot of trash. • The rotting waste produces gases that can be harnessed to create gas or electrical power.	• Limited amounts of suitable land available. • The waste can seep out and pollute soils and groundwater in the area. • The rotting waste produces gases that can explode.
Incinerator (burn it) 	• Reduces 85–90% of the trash to ash.	• Requires the building of a big incinerator. • Can send smoke and ash into the air as well as **toxic** gases that contribute to **acid rain**.
Composting (let it rot back into the soil) 	• Clean – doesn't produce any toxins. • No waste – everything rots down. • Results in rich compost that can be sold to people to help them grow plants.	• **Labor-intensive** – waste needs to be sorted first to get rid of items that won't rot down, then trash is usually ground up so that it rots faster.

Over the years, it has become obvious that trash never really goes away, and it usually has an impact on the place where it ends up. Fish in rivers near landfills have died from the poisons that seep out of the ground into the water. Forests have died because of poisonous gases in the air, often from chimneys that burn waste. People living in houses built near old landfills have been in danger from leaking gases.

So some people began thinking of other ways to deal with trash. Some companies started working on ways to recycle used products into new products.

Other people started to think of ways to make something *different* out of trash. Could a plastic soda bottle become part of a shirt?

Could a whole pile of garbage provide power for hundreds of homes? Could rubber *on* the road be made into rubber *in* the road? And what could be done with astronauts' dirty underwear?

This book is about some of the thousands of bright ideas (and very successful businesses) that have grown out of people's thoughts on how to turn trash – stuff that *used* to be something useful – into something useful again. That's the process called RECYCLING.

Used to new

- Used paper goes into new paper and cardboard items – and even house insulation.
- Used plastic items are broken down and made into different new plastic items.

- Glass from used bottles is added to glass in new bottles.
- Used lead acid batteries are crushed and melted to make new batteries.
- Used aluminum cans are melted down into new aluminum products.

2. From Bottles to Clothes

Not many people look at a plastic soda bottle and think about what clothing they could make from it.

But somebody did, and in 1993, an American company announced that they had found a way to spin soda bottles into fiber – soft, fleecy fiber that could be made into thermal underwear, sweaters, socks, jeans, and fleece jackets.

The manufacturers had discovered that making fiber out of recycled soda bottles not only uses up some of our hard-to-get-rid-of trash but also uses less energy than chemically manufactured fiber and creates less air pollution.

From bottles to clothing

Soda bottles are sent to recycling center and sorted.

Bottles are cleaned, purified, and chopped into small flakes.

Flakes are melted, **extruded**, and spun into polyester fiber.

Fiber is made into fabric and sent to clothing manufacturer.

Fabric is made into clothing and other fleecy products.

Bottle fabric facts

- Soda bottles used to make fleece or denim clothes are made from PET (PolyEthylene Terephthalate).
- 10 PET bottles are used to make about 1 pound of new fiber.
- 2.5 million plastic soda bottles are thrown out every hour in the United States. That equals 60 million each day or 2.19 billion per year.
- Plastic soda bottles make up 5% of all plastic waste.

By using PET bottles in their fabric process, companies claim that in 2 years, they have:
- recycled 4.8 billion bottles
- saved 1.3 million barrels of oil
- eliminated 749,000 tons of harmful air emissions.

3. The Stinky Smelly Stuff

Trash that is dumped, piled up, or compacted rots pretty fast. And if you've ever found a pile of old apple cores under your bed, you'll know that rotting things *smell*. This is because, as they rot, food and other substances give off a mixture of gases, including methane. (People and animals make methane too; it pops out of us when we "break wind.")

The process of rotting is also called decomposition. Decomposition is where things break down and return to the air or the earth.

The problem with methane is that it is one of the greenhouse gases that can damage our environment and contribute to global warming.

Some of the human activities that increase the amount of greenhouse gases in the atmosphere

Some of the heat from the Sun is reflected back into space

Greenhouse gases trap some of the heat from the Sun

Earth absorbs heat from the Sun

Cars release carbon monoxide

Destroying forests means there is more carbon dioxide in the air

Farming produces methane

Burning fossil fuels such as coal, oil, and natural gas releases carbon dioxide

Household and industrial activities produce CFCs (chlorofluorocarbons)

Greenhouse gases such as carbon dioxide and methane trap heat from the Sun and warm Earth's atmosphere. The amount of gases in the atmosphere has greatly increased in the last 150 years due to human activity. This means that more heat is being trapped in the atmosphere, and this is causing Earth's temperature to rise. Scientists call this global warming.

Methane can also be dangerous because it is **flammable**. Methane can leak out from rotting areas like landfills and creep underground into basements and pits and under drain covers. There it mixes with air, and if a spark or flame comes in contact with it, BOOM! The gas can explode.

The good news about methane is that it is *useful*. In some cities, methane from landfills is used to generate electricity. For example, a landfill site in Texas is generating electricity that powers more than 6,500 homes.

In New Zealand, gas collection experts discovered that piping the gas *direct* to homes and businesses can produce about three times as much energy as generating electricity on site.

Bores are drilled into the waste pile, and the methane is pumped out and tested. If it's not good quality or there's not much of it, the gas is "flared" off (burned, releasing **carbon dioxide** and water) so that it's not hanging around, which could be dangerous. But if the gas is good quality and there is lots of it, the next steps are:

- The landfill is covered with plastic to stop the gas escaping.
- More bores are drilled and are connected up to pipes underneath the plastic.

Methane gas processing plant

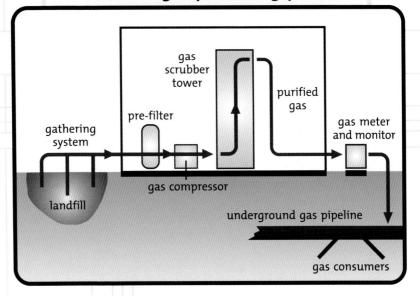

- The pipes carry the gas to a processing plant on site.
- At the processing plant, the gas is "scrubbed" (treated to get rid of **impurities** and excess carbon dioxide).
- The clean methane is pumped through underground pipes to homes and businesses, where it can be used in gas appliances as an alternative to **natural gas**.

About those underpants

Getting methane from landfills is a big-scale project, but here's a small-scale one that Russian scientists are working on.

Imagine you're an astronaut at the **Mir Space Station**. You're wearing a spacesuit and ... underwear. There are no washing machines around, and you know that waste is a big problem in space – you and your fellow astronauts are already creating around 6 pounds of uncompressed waste each day.

The waste is bagged up and handed back to the supply **module** when it visits about twice a year. The module burns up as it reenters Earth's atmosphere.

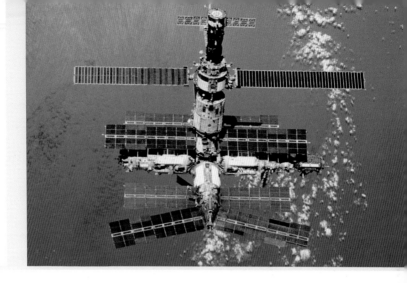

So, if you're like most astronauts, you'll wear your underwear for about a week before you add it to the growing pile of waste, and try not to worry about the health hazards of all that stuff rotting on board.

BUT ... Russian scientists are designing a mix of bacteria that will "eat" underwear, plastic, and **organic waste**. The bacteria will speed up the rotting process and, just like in a landfill, the rotting process will create methane. And methane, as we now know, is a very useful fuel, which could be used to power spacecraft.

So watch out for that space mission to Mars – powered by the crew's dirty underwear!

4. *Worm Work*

How would you like to share your lunch with worms? This is what a group of elementary school students are doing. About 1,000 worms live in a worm farm in the schoolyard. The students and teachers eat their lunches, and the worms eat the leftovers. The worms recycle the leftovers into a nutritious compost that makes good food for plants. The plants grow big and strong. The students eat the plants. The worms eat the leftovers ... and so on.

This is how it started:

Each week, two students were chosen to be Green Hands. Their job was to empty all the leftovers into the compost bins. There are three compost bins in the yard – one for fresh food scraps, one for rotted-down food scraps, and one for the food scraps that are so rotted down they are just like soil, only full of "food" for plants. This soil is used on the garden.

Then the students found out that worms make the compost even better, so the school bought a worm bin (made from 100 percent recycled plastic). It has a top (working) bin where the worms go and a bottom bin where the stuff for the garden ends up. Compost is used to make the "bedding" for the worms to go into.

The students ordered some worms, which came in the mail – 1,000 reddish brown, wriggly red worms packed in a cardboard cylinder.

The students put the worm bedding into the top bin and placed the worms in one corner. Then they put handfuls of food scraps on top of the bedding for the worms to eat. They put newspaper and cardboard on top of the food to keep the worms warm and damp.

Now that the worm farm is set up,
this is what happens:

On Mondays, Wednesdays, and Fridays, some
of the food scraps are sorted out and
chopped up to go into the worm farm. The
worms can't be fed citrus fruit or meat
because they won't eat citrus (it's too acidic)
and meat attracts flies.

The worms eat the food scraps, and the
resulting waste products are called
worm castings.

The students sprinkle the worm castings
around the plants or pour water through
the worm farm so that the castings dissolve
and drip into the bottom bin. Then they
pull out the bottom bin and use the liquid in
it to feed the plants – it makes really
concentrated plant food, so they have to
add water to it first.

Then the students can eat the plants –
they're growing peas, beans, and strawberries
– and they can sell them at the school
fair, too.

Best of all, the worms lay eggs that hatch
into *more* worms to make *more* compost
that can grow *more* plants. The students
just have to remember to keep feeding the
worms – and to buy another working bin
to put on top of the first working bin so
that there is enough space for the worms
to live in.

Top (working) bin contains compost, food scraps, and worms

Bottom bin collects liquid containing dissolved worm castings

Worm farm facts

- Worms like dark, cool, moist places; not too wet, not too dry. They need air to breathe.
- Composting worms are best suited for worm farms because they have big appetites, are fast breeders, and like the moist conditions. The most common composting worm is the red worm.
- Composting worms breed every 7–10 days, so the population in a worm farm will double in 2–3 months.
- Composting worms can eat about half their body weight in one day.
- If a worm farm becomes too crowded, the worms will stop breeding until some of them are removed.

When the rubber meets the road

Rubber, like plastic, is very useful until you want to get rid of it. Rubber doesn't break down easily (which is great when it's on your car or bike), and if you try to bury a rubber tire in a landfill, it tends to rise to the surface.

Rubber facts

- Rubber is made from latex, the milky sap of the rubber tree.

- Natural latex is waterproof, springy, and easily molded into shapes.

- Natural latex becomes gluey very quickly, so if you want to make something with it, you have to do it on the spot – then it lasts well. But if you soften it by using heat or chemicals or by grinding, it loses its strength.

- In the mid-19th century, inventor Charles Goodyear was trying to find a way to treat latex rubber so that it would stay strong, smooth, and springy. He accidentally dropped some on a hot stove. It didn't melt. It charred like leather. Goodyear had made the first piece of **vulcanized** rubber!

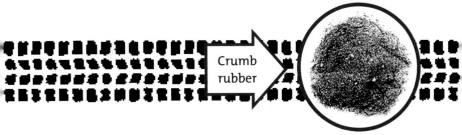

Crumb rubber

Tires are made from rubber and chemicals that are vulcanized by heat into a product that is very hard to break down.

About 257 million tires (about one tire per person in the United States) are scrapped each year.

Some of them can be reused as **retreads**, some are burned to produce energy, and about 600,000 are recycled into other products. At first, this was costly and used a lot of energy. Then a company in Puerto Rico invented the crumb rubber process:

- The rubber is shredded into chips.
- The chips are frozen.
- The frozen chips are hammered into crumbs.
- The crumbs are separated out from the bits of steel and fluff.

Crumb rubber is used in:
- roads (mixed with asphalt)
- tires
- sports surfaces, such as running tracks, tennis courts, and safety mats for schoolyards
- shoes – including sneakers, construction boots, and hiking boots.

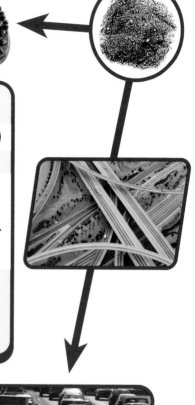

The oily hair solution

In 1989, an Alabama hairdresser watched a TV news item about the disastrous oil spill from the oil tanker *Exxon Valdez*. The TV coverage showed the rescue of an otter whose sleek, hairy coat had become soaked in oil.

"If the hair on an otter can soak up oil," the hairdresser thought, "I wonder how much oil the hair from my salon floor could soak up?"

He poured some motor oil into his son's wading pool, then he filled an old pair of tights with some of the hair from the floor of his salon. He dipped the tights into the pool. Slurp! The hair soaked up the oil. The hairdresser took his idea to NASA. Now NASA engineers are working to develop a hair-based oil **filter** to clean up oil spills.

It costs about 50 cents per liter to clean up spilled oil using a hair filter compared with about $2.50 per liter to clean up oil using conventional methods, such as detergents.

A corker idea

Corks are really useful to stop liquid pouring out of bottles. Bottles are often recycled, but corks are usually thrown out. However, in Australia, corks are collected and sent to a cork recycling company that pays by the pound for cork (which makes people want to collect and send more).

The company grinds up the corks into small granules that are used in industrial safety mats, flooring for horse floats, and the insides of cricket balls.

Cork comes from the cork oak tree. When the tree is about 30 years old, the outside bark layer of the tree is stripped off and made into corks. Then the tree has to grow new bark, which takes about 9 years.

Glossary

(These words are printed in bold type
the first time they appear in the book.)

acid rain: rain containing acid
formed mainly from
industrial waste gases;
acid rain causes damage
to lakes and rivers, trees,
people, and buildings

bore: a hole that is made with
a cutting tool or machine

carbon dioxide: a colorless, odorless gas
that occurs naturally in
the atmosphere and
when mammals
breathe out

extruded: forced out through tiny
nozzles to make thin
threads

filter: a sieve to strain liquids

flammable:	easily set on fire
impurities:	in methane, substances that are not pure methane
labor-intensive:	a task that requires a lot of workers
Mir Space Station:	a space laboratory put into orbit by Russia in 1986
module:	the self-contained unit of a spacecraft
natural gas:	a colorless, odorless gas that is produced by drilling into Earth's crust
organic waste:	naturally occurring waste
retreads:	tires that have a new tread
toxic:	poisonous
vulcanization:	the process of treating rubber with heat in order to increase its strength

Index